VAUCLUSE

Avignon • Ventoux • Orange • Luberon

Text written
in association
with Gabrielle Silver

▲ *The Mont Ventoux.*

◀ *Mornas Castle. At the end of the 12th century it fell into the hands of the Counts of Toulouse. Under Catholic control during the Wars of Religion, it was beseiged by the Huguenots in 1512. The attackers, led by Dupuy of Montbrun, forced their victims to jump from the cliff.*

▶ *Valréas, the Simiane Mansion. In 1317, pope John XXII purchased the town from the Dauphin John II, a first step in creating the Enclave of the Popes.*

▲▲ *The Barry. North of Bollène, this village of cave dwellings occupies the site of an ancient Celtic oppidum.*

▲ *Saignon, a village situated north of the Mourre Nègre. At 1125 meters of altitude, it is the highest point of the Luberon Mountain.*

LAND OF PROVENCE

The *Vallis Clausa,* the Closed Valley, where one finds the famous spring, gave its name to the department of the Vaucluse which was created by the Convention on June 25, 1793. This department is demarcated by the Durance River to the south, by the Rhône to the west, and by the Aigues to the north, where it brims over into the triangle formed by Caderousse, Bollène and Saint-Cécile-le-Vignes. To the east its border skirts northward round Vaison-la-Romaine, missing the Baronnies, then passing between the Mont Ventoux and Lure Mountain. It then crosses the Albion plateau, to the east of the Vaucluse plateau, follows the course of the Calavon River from the Opedette Canyon, crosses this river to the west of Céreste and borders the eastern flank of the Great Luberon before connecting with the Durance at its confluence with the Verdon. The Vaucluse also integrates the canton of Valréas, enclosed in the department of the Drome to the north. Two lords rule the region: the Rhône and the Mistral. The first enters untamed at the Donzère-Mondragon Pass, a strategic point surveyed by the Mornas Castle, half way between Bollène and Orange, and receives reinforcements from the Ardèche, the Aygues, the Ouvèze and the Durance. The second, master of the winds, emerges from the furrow traced by the Rhône River and unfurls in gusts which can attain two hundred and fifty kilometres an

hour. The earth here is rich, favored by a temperate climate. There are many vineyards; those of the Côtes du Rhône, but also those of the Luberon and the Enclave of the Popes. The Comtat Venaissin is a market gardening centre, while melons have become virtually synonymous with Cavaillon. If lavender prefers the rocky soil of Haute Provence, its cultivation is concentrated on the plateau of Valensole, south of the plateau of Vaucluse, in the region of Sault. The olive tree flourishes along the southern side of the mountains and Nyons, renowned for its olive oil, is not far from Vaison-la-Romaine. Even the "black diamond", the truffle, is harvested here, at the foot of oak trees in Tricastin and the Luberon. In December, the farmer's market of Richerenche is bustling. Over the centuries, this land has witnessed the passage and clash of Celts, Phocaeans, Romans, Barbarians, Saracens and Franks successively. After having been a part of the Lotharingian empire, and the Marquisate of Provence from the 9th to the 11th century, its territory was parcelled out between the Comtat Venaissin, Avignon and the Principality of Orange from the 13th to the 11th century. Although the principality became a part of the Kingdom of France through the treaty of Utrecht in 1713, it wasn't until 1791 that Avignon and the Comtat were annexed to France. Only in 1814 did the papacy officially accept the loss of territory that had been in its possession for five centuries.

▲ *Chateauneuf-du-Pape, the cellar of father Anselme, 14th century cask in the museum of wine-grower's tools. Created by the popes during the 14th century, the vineyard of Chateauneuf-du-Pape profits from a microclimate produced when the riverstones from the alluvial terrace of the Rhône store daylight heat. They then release this heat at night, allowing the grapes to reach a high degree of maturity. Today, the quality of the red and white wine is guaranteed by an A.O.C.*

▶ *The Pont Julien, this sixty-eight metre long bridge was built on the Calavon River during the 1st century B.C. Its name probably derives from its proximity to the former Roman colony Apta Julia, the town of Apt, located only a few kilometres up river.*

▲ *Field of lavender near Sault; Lavender was wellknown for its curative properties and its characteristic fragrance that gave a fresh scent to washes. Its name derives from the latin "lavare", to wash. For a long time it was gathered in the wild before it was cultivated, for the first time, at the beginning of the 20th century.*

▼ *The Berlingots (hard candy) from Carpentras. Provence has a longstanding tradition of dessert and sweet-making. It was in Carpentras, in 1851 that the confectioner Eysseric invented the Berlingot .*

5

▲ *Avignon, the Pont Saint-Bénézat and Saint Nicolas Chapel with the Ventoux in the backround. Contrary to the refrain from the popular song, it was on Barthelasse Island, over which the bridge passes, and not on the bridge itself that dances would take place. The legend tells how in 1177, an angel asked the young shepard Bénézat to build a bridge across the Rhône. To convince the doubtful, the child effortlessly lifted an enormous rock. The work was finished in eleven year's times. Composed of twenty-two arches, the bridge was rebuilt during the 13th century and reinforced two centuries later. But the Rhône is merciless and washed away an entire section during the 17th century.*

▶ *Avignon, the Palace of the Popes.*

AVIGNON

▲ *Avignon, the ramparts. Built between 1359 and 1371, they were intended to protect the city as much from the river's moods as from the roving highwaymen who coveted its riches.*

▼ *Avignon, the Palace of the Popes, paving of Benoît XII's studium. This former bishop of Fontfroide had the Old Palace built which, by its austere style, characterized the Cistercian order to which he belonged.*

T he Celto-Ligurians called their village *Aouennio* when they settled on what is now called the rocher des Doms, the Doms' Rock, which stands on the left bank of the Rhône between the confluences of the Ouvèze and the Durance Rivers. A Massalian trading post before becoming a *civitas* of the Narbonnaise, located on the *Via Agrippa*, Avignon suffered the raids and razzias of the Vandals, the Visigoths, the Burgondes and the Ostrogoths before being ousted by the Franks who obliterated all traces of the *Pax Romana*. In 735, the city was invaded by the Saracens only to be recaptured by Charles Martel in 741. In 1125, it was part of the Marquisate of Provence, fief of the Counts of Toulouse. Because of Avignon's loyalty to its suzerain, Raymond VII, it was beseiged by the troops of Louis VIII on his royal crusade to Catharistic Languedoc. Meanwhile, the legend recounts how Bénézat, following the angel's request , built a wooden bridge measuring nine hundred metres long across the Rhône. Decidedly rebellious, Avignon formed a confederacy with Arles and Marseille against the House of Anjou in 1241 only to be forced back into submission in 1251. Under the influence of Philip the Fair, Clément V established the papacy in Avignon in 1309. Seven popes resided on French soil between 1309 and 1376. The Palace of Popes was built during the pontificate of Benoit XII and Clément VI, from 1334 to 1363. But the

city did not become official property of the Holy See until 1348, when Clément VI purchased it from Queen Jeanne of Naples, Countess of Provence, for eighty thousand gold florins. The plague struck the city that same year. One of its victims was Petrarque's muse, the beautiful Laura of Noves, whom he had first met in Avignon in 1327. The presence of the pontificale court brought about the city's golden age. Religious men and penitents, artists and merchants made Avignon their centre, spreading its reputation far and wide. In January of 1377, the Holy See returned to Rome. It was the end of an era, even if two antipopes, Clément VII and Bénoit XIII, remained on the banks of the Rhône until 1408. From then on, Avignon was administered by Papale Legates and experienced more trails and tribulations: it was occupied twice by Louis XIV and in 1791 the population was decimated by the plague brought from Marseille the same year it was annexed to France by the Constituent Assembly. From its past, Avignon has received a rich architectural heritage which includes, in addition to the Palace of the Popes, Notre-Dame-des-Doms, the Mint and many churches. The Calvet and Petit-Palais Museums are two of the city's many museums. And each year, from the second week of July to the first week of August, the festival of Dramatic Arts created by Jean Vilar in 1947 takes place in the city streets.

Avignon, the Palace of
[th]e Popes, the Great Tinel.
[Be]fore it was partially
[de]stroyed in the fire of 1413,
[thi]s reception room's ceiling
[wa]s strung with a midnight
[blu]e linen cloth, embroidered
[wi]th gold stars.

Avignon, the Palace of the
[Po]pes, the pope's bedchamber.

► Avignon, the Palace
[of] the Popes, fresco from
[th]e Stag Room, the private
[ch]ambers of Clément VI,
[th]e pope who had the
[Pa]lais-Neuf built next to
[th]e Palais-Vieux.

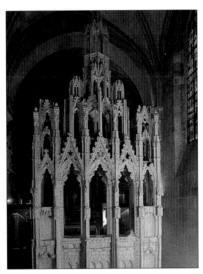

◄◄ Avignon, Notre-Dame-
des-Doms. This cathedral,
the oldest religious edifice
in Avignon, underwent
many transformations over
the centuries: originally
Romanesque, it was enlarged
during the 14th century and
acquired a Baroque façade
during the 17th century.

◄ Avignon, Notre-Dame-des-
Doms, the tomb of Jean XXII.
Originally from Cahors,
Jacques Duèse was bishop
of Avignon before being
elected pope in 1316.
He had Thomas Aquinas
canonized in 1323.

Avignon, the Petit-Palais
[M]useum, Virgin and Child
[by] Botticelli.

Avignon, the Petit-Palais
[M]useum, the kidnapping
[of] Hélène de Liberale da
[Ve]rona. Napoleon III
[pu]rchased certain works
[fr]om the Marquis
[C]ampana, a nobleman
[co]nvicted for embezzlement.

► Avignon, the Petit-
[P]alais Museum, Saint
[C]atherine of Sienna.

Avignon, the Calvet
[M]useum, bas-relief from
[C]abrières.

◄ *Villeneuve-lès-Avignon,*
Philippe le Bel Tower.
The Rhône was Capetian
property. When the river
flooded the lower section of
Avignon, its inhabitants
were considered to be in
France and were obligated
to pay taxes to its king.

▼ *Villeneuve-lès-Avignon,*
the Municipal Museum:
The Coronation of the Virgin
by Enguerrand Quarton.
Discovered by Mérimée in
1834, this masterpiece from
the Avignon School was
painted in 1453.

◄◄ *Villeneuve-lès-Avignon, the Charterhouse, the Rotunda. Located in the cloisters of Saint-Jean, it shelters the basin of an 18th century fountain.*

◄ *Villeneuve-lès-Avignon, the Charterhouse, a fresco painted by Matteo Giovannetti in the chapel of the "livrée" which belonged to Etienne Aubert.*

▼ *Villeneuve-lès-Avignon, entrance to fort Saint-André. A Benedictine abbey and the village of Saint-André used to be found within its surrounding wall.*

VILLENEUVE-LÈS-AVIGNON

When Philippe III le Hardi acquired the County of Toulouse at the death of Alphonse of Poitiers in 1271, his kingdom reached the right bank of the Rhône. Henceforth, only the river seperated the Crown lands from those of the County of Provence, acting as a natural border. Philip the Fair founded a new town opposite Avignon. Aware of its strategic position, he had a tower built on the rock serving as the bridgehead of Saint-Bénézet. The arrival of the papacy in Avignon was a godsend for the "new town". Too cramped inside the corset of ramparts in the papal city, the cardinals crossed the bridge. There they built fourteen *livrées*, sumptuous residences worthy of their rank, including the one which belonged to cardinal Étienne Aubert who became pope in 1352 under the name Innocent VI. Elected as a result of the withdrawal of candidature of the general of the Carthusians, he donated his *livrée* to this order in the Val de Bénédiction, and founded a Charterhouse there where he asked to be buried. Military defense remained a priority and Jean le Bon and Charles V had Fort André built on Mount Andaon. Construction lasted between 1362 and 1368. In 1382, a nineteen year old cardinal named Pierre de Luxembourg died in the odour of sanctity. Today, his *livrée* houses the rich collections of the Municipal Museum.

11

ORANGE

▲ *Orange, Triumphal*
Arch. On the Via Agrippa
which linked Lyon to Arles…

Orange, detail on the
Triumphal Arch: outfitting
Roman ships.

Orange, the scenic wall
of the Roman Theatre.
Louis XIV had exclaimed
"it is the most beautiful
wall in my kingdom".

Orange, Municipal
Museum, fragments from
the cadastres of Orange.
All things were located
using the axes "cardo"
and "decamanus".

O n the Aigues River, *Arausio* was
home to the Celtic Tricastini.
According to Livy, it was near
this village that the cimbri and
Teutons scattered the Roman army in 120 B.C.
In 102 B.C., Marius repaired the damages by
defeating the barbarians near *Aquae Sextiae,*
the future Aix-en-Provence. Around 35 B.C.,
Orange became a retirement colony for
veterens of the Gallica legion and in 21 B.C.
those of the Augusta legion began arriving
around the same time that Orange achieved
the status of Roman colony under the name
colonia Julia Secundanorum. The colony and its
surrounding territory were surveyed and
registered according to a strict cadastral map
engraved in marble tablets. In his *Naturalis*
Historia, Pliny referred to the city as one of the
largest of those in the *Narbonensis.* Gradually, it
acquired a host of monuments; the Triumphal
Arch for example, built during the 1st century,
and the Roman Theatre, from the beginning
of the 2nd century, with its *cavea* of tiers which
could hold up to 10,000 spectators. In 406,
Orange was invaded by the Alamans and the
Wisigoths did the same in 410. During the
11th century, the city became capital of an
county enclaved in the Comtat Venaissin. In
1181, the Earl of Orange was conferred the
title of prince by Emperor Frederic. Fief to the
House of Baux for a time, the county passed
into the hands of the Nassaus of Holland in
1544 before it was annexed to France in 1713.

▲▲ *Vaison-la-Romaine, House of the Silver Bust.*

▲ *Vaison-la-Romaine, the Théo-Desplans Archeological Museum, the silver bust of a patrician. This museum houses the finds from the excavations carried out on the site, such as those undertaken in 1907 by the abbot Joseph Sautel in the Villasse and Puymin sections.*

▲ *Vaison-la-Romaine, mosaic, from the Peacock Villa. The city was describ[ed] as an "urbs opulentissima[?]" by the historian Pomponi[us] Mela.*

◀ *Vaison-la-Romaine, the portico of Pompey. Now on view at the Théo-Desplans Museum, these statues of Hadrien and Sabine adorned its galleries.*

▶ *Vaison-la-Romaine, the Saint Quenin Chapel. Although it was built during the 12th century, much older fragments were used in its construction.*

VAISON-LA-ROMAINE

On the banks of the Ouvèze River, *Vasio Vocontiorum* was the capital of the Voconces, the Celtic tribe which, in 125 B.C., defeated the Roman legions led by Fulvius Flaccus along with those led by Sextius Calvinus one year later. The *Provincia* was created by the Romans in 120 B.C. Between 69 and 59 B.C., Vaison became a *civitas fœderata*, a federated city, linked to Rome by a treaty called a *fœdus* which accorded a great autonomy to the city while imposing submission to the Republic. With the advent of the Empire in 27 B.C. and during the *Pax Romana*, Vaison prospered through commerce and trade. Goatskins filled with wine, gallic wheat or Italian goods were transported on rafts down the Ouvèze, crossable by a single-arched bridge. Large *villæ* were built as the city grew to over sixty hectares. Gardens, thermae and fountains were fitted up around opulent *domus* and in a temple from the Augustinian period, the imperial cult was worshipped. In the 1st century A.D., a theatre was built against the Puymin Hill. The Gallic elite were able to climb the rungs of civil and religious honours, thereby gaining Roman citizenship and rubbing shoulders with influential people of the Empire. There was Burrus, for example, Nero's private tutor, who came to live in Vaison. In 313, the Edict of Milan proclaimed freedom of worship and within the year Vaison became the seat of a bishopric.

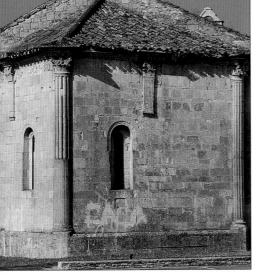

▲ *The Dentelles of Montmirail, otherwise called the Dentelles Sarrasines.*

◄ *Crestet, a small street.*

► *Notre-Dame d'Aubune. The chapel was built during the 9th and the 10th century and its bell tower added on a century later.*

▼ *Séguret, the 12th century church.*

*Le Barroux with its castle
~~an~~d the Ventoux as a
~~ba~~ckdrop.*

*Carpentras, the Triumphal
~~Ar~~ch, bas-relief representing
~~tw~~o captives chained to
~~tro~~phies. This monument
~~wa~~s built in 20 B.C.*

*Carpentras, the Saint
~~Sif~~frein Cathedral, the
~~sou~~thern portal, otherwise
~~cal~~led the Jewish Door.*

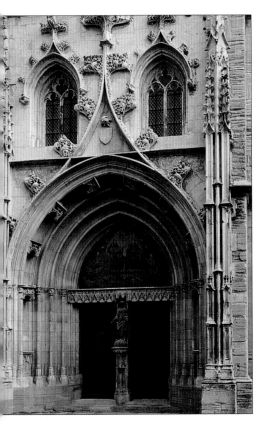

AT THE FOOT OF THE VENTOUX

By passed to the North by the Ouvèze and to the south by the Nesque, the Ventoux dominates the surrounding plain at 1912 meters of altitude. West of its cone, the **Dentelles of Montmirail** display their jagged ridge of Jurassic limestone. Hikers can discover the marked paths in the heart of the surrounding massifs: the Cayron to the north, the Grand Montmirail , the Clapis, the Salle to the south. They are surrounded by a group of villages such as **Crestet**, **Séguret** or Suzette. A section of the ramparts built by the princes of Orange still stands in Gigondas where the wine has acquired a well-deserved reputation. Near Beaumes-de-Venise stands the Romanesque **Notre-Dame d'Aubune** Chapel. During the 12th century, the Lords of Baux had a castle built in **Barroux** which was transformed into a Renaissance dwelling between 1539 and 1549. Today, it houses the Centre for Historical and Archeological Studies of the Comtat. A few kilometres from the village, the Benedictine monastery Sainte-Madeleine was established as an abbey in 1989. To the south, the Auzon River runs through **Carpentras,** which was the capital of the Méminians, a Celtic tribe. During the 1st century B.C. it became a Roman colony, *Forum Neronis,* named for Julius Caesar's lieutenant. The Marquisate of Provence entered the sphere of influence of the Counts of Toulouse in 1125; in 1229 the Holy-See acquired the city through the treaty

of Meaux. In 1313, Clement V sojourned in Carpentras which became the capital of the Comtat in 1320. During the same period, Jews driven from France by Philip the Fair took refuge in Carpentras. To the east, the cemetary in **Mazan** has preserved around sixty Gallo-Roman sarcophagi. Near Malaucène flows the Groseau Spring which the Romans canalized by aqueduct all the way to Vaison. It was upon the ruins of a Mérovingian monastery that had been destroyed by the Saracens in 683 that the monks of Saint-Victor of Marseille built the chapel of **Notre-Dame du Groseau** during the 11th century. Clement V later chose it to be his summer residence. The traditional ascent of the Ventoux is made by a road which begins in Bédoin and becomes quite steep between Saint-Estève, le Chalet-Reynard and its summit. Down-river from Sault, the **Nesque** River carved gorges out of the Plateau of Vaucluse. In **Méthamis**, one can see the remains of a wall built in 1720 to halt the spread of the plague. **Venasque**, *Vindusca*, which is on the ancient road which led from Apt to Carpentras, gave its name to the Comtat. Its 6th century baptistery is one of the oldest religious edifices in France. Before joining with the Sorgue River, the Nesque passes through **Pernes-les-Fontaines**, aptly named, for it has no less than thirty fountains. Capital of the Comtat from 968 to 1320, the city has preserved the frescoes painted in 1280 in its Ferrande Tower.

▲▲ *Notre-Dame du Groseau, the vauclusian spring.*

▲ *Notre-Dame du Groseau.*

▶ *Méthamis, the plague wall, built to halt the spread of the plague in 1720.*

◀ *The Nesque Gorges, the Cire Rock.*

▶ *Mazan. Gallo-Roman sarcophagi.*

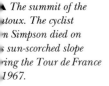

▲ *The summit of the [Ven]toux. The cyclist [To]m Simpson died on [thi]s sun-scorched slope [du]ring the Tour de France [in] 1967.*

Venasque. The baptistery, [the] floorplan is in the form [of a] Greek cross.

Pernes-les-Fontaines, [the] frescoes in the Ferrande [Tow]er: battle of knights.

▲ *Fontaine-de-Vaucluse, the reappearance of the Sorgue. The spring's rate of flow is measured by a graduated scale called a "sorgometre". Averaging fifteen cubic metres per second, it can reach up to two hundred cubic metres per second.*

◄ *L'Isle-sur-la-Sorgue, a paddle wheel. During the 19th century, there we seventy of them in use.*

▶ *The Thouzon Cave. Discovered in 1902, it contains fistulous rocks and other cave formation*

▲▲ *Fontaine-de-Vaucluse, the Vallis Clausa Mill, paper drying. Since 1981, "hand made" paper has been manufactured in this mill using traditional methods from the 15th century.*

▲ *Fontaine-de-Vaucluse, modillions on Saint Véran Church.*

FONTAINE-DE-VAUCLUSE

At the far end of a valley, at the foot of a cirque of rocky cliffs, the emerald waters of the Sorgue emerge from a deep cavity to the light of day. This site has become a reference in hydrology since "vauclusian fountain" is the term used to designate a resurgent spring. The abundance of its flow as well as its consistancy, even during periods of drought, cannot be solely explained by the rainwater filtered off the surface of the plateau of Vaucluse, the Nesque basin or the slopes of the Ventoux. The abyss has been explored several times; by captain Cousteau in 1957 and in 1985, the – 308 metre mark was reached. But was this really the bottom? The *Vallis Clausa* was occupied and deified by the Romans, who built a canal there to transport the waters of the Sorgue all the way to Arles. During the 6th century, the hermit Véran settled in the valley and rid it of the *Coulobre*, a monster that was terrorizing the region. The church consecrated in his name, containing a crypt with his tomb, was built in the 11th century. In the 14th century, it was in this "charming valley" that Petrarch found the calm he needed to compose his love poem to Laura, the *Canzonierre*. In Fontaine-de-Vaucluse, as well as down-river in **L'Isle-sur-la-Sorgue**, the river waters made many millwheels turn. While to the north, other waters still, underground this time, carved the rock to create the **Thouzon Cave**.

SÉNANQUE

I n 1148, twelve monks from the Cistercian abbey in Mazan settled in the northern part of the Luberon in the narrow valley of the Sénancole River on land given to them by the Lords of Simiane, suzerains of Gordes. The construction of the abbey-church began in 1160 and was completed at the beginning of the 13th century. The sobriety of its architecture corresponds with the Cistercian will to banish splendour and pomp in their abbeys, as clearly explained by Bernard de Clairvaux. During the 13th century, new members flooded in and their domain grew, through numerous donations, from the south of the Dauphiné to the plateau of Albion and from the Luberon all the way to Marseille and Arles. Recruits became rarer during the 15th century but Jean Casaletti, the abbot from 1475 to 1509, took charge of the abbey and founded the college of Saint-Bernard of Sénanque in Avignon. In 1544, led by the parish priest of Ménerbes, the Waldenses pillaged and set fire to the abbey which fell into a slow decline until the Revolution. It was then sold as national property. In 1854, the abbot Barnouin set up his community here and in 1858 it became affiliated with the order of Cîteaux. In 1872, this community, after having repopulated the abbeys of Fontfroide and Lérins, became the Congregation of the Immaculate Conception of Sénanque. Twice evicted, in 1880 and in 1903, the monks have returned to Sénanque since 1988.

▲ *Sénanque, squinch
of the transept crossing.
The dome on squinches
of the abbey-church of
Sénanque is a reminder
of the one at the mother-
abbey of Mazan in Velay.*

*Sénanque, the south
transept and the tomb of
the Lord of Venasque.*

◀ *Sénanque, the cloisters.*

*Sénanque, the
Tarasque, a legendary
amphibious monster,
sculpture on a console of
the north galerie of the
cloisters.*

▲ *Gordes. At its summit stands the castle renovated by Bertrand of Simiane, nicknamed "the French Epaminondas" for his courage in diplomacy.*

▼ *The Lavander Museum. During the summer, lavender, or more often a hybrid lavender, is picked, dried, and then distilled. A hundred kilograms of hybrid lavender produces only one kilogram of essence.*

GORDES

On the fringe of the plateau of Vaucluse, the houses of Gordes rise in terraces along the slopes of a rocky knoll crowned by the Saint Firmin Church, with its campanile on top, and the castle of the Agoult-Simiane. The Romans certainly occupied these heights and in the 12th century the Lords of Agoult built a fortified castle here which was reinforced during the 14th century and restructured during the 16th century by Bertrand de Simiane. At the end of a large room, an imposing fireplace dates back to 1541. A helical staircase, a remarkable specimen of stereotomy, the science of cutting solids, leads to the third floor. To the south-west of Gordes, the **Bories village** presents a group of drystone constructions. This *architecture of necessity* uses a building material readily available in the region, limestone *lauzes*, which are assembled without mortar. The walls, the framework and the roof are formed by stones around ten centimetres thick. They are placed one on top of the the other and moved slightly forward to create a corbelled vault as a watertight summital slab. Between Gordes and Beaumettes, in Bois Castle, a museum is dedicated entirely to lavender. And not far away, on the edge of the Luberon Regional Natural Park, the Romanesque chapel of **Saint-Pantaléon**, built during the 12th century, watches over its stone necropolis.

▲ *Saint-Pantaléon, the rock necropolis at the foot of the east-end of the Romanesque chapel. Most of the tombs are no larger than the size of a small child, suggesting that it was used as a "sanctuary of respite": according to the belief, a child who had died before being baptized, if buried here, would be received in the kingdom of heaven.*

◀ *Gordes, the Bories village. The name "Bories" comes from the latin word baoria, for a cowshed. Used as cabins, toolsheds, sheepfolds or farms, they are found individually or grouped together in the Lure Mountain, on the slopes of the Ventoux and in the Luberon region. The drystone construction technique was perfected in the Neolithic age but the Bories found in Gordes are thought to be between 200 and 500 years old.*

▲ *The Colorado of Rustre*
Once the flowers of ochre
have been obtained throug
washing and drying, the
combination of oxides in t
powders produces a great
variety of colors. These
pigments were used by ma
to decorate cave walls as
early as the Palaeolithic a

◄ *Roussillon. Mount*
Ventoux in the backround

▶ *Apt, the silhouette of*
Saint Anne Cathedral
emerging from the rooftops
the town, with its belltower
campanile and dome atop
the transept crossing.

▲ *Apt, Saint Anne Cathedral, the treasure: arabic standard, woven in Damiette in 1097 and brought back from the Holy Land by the crusaders.*

▼ *Apt, the Municipal Museum: earthenware boiling pot.*

▼▼ *Apt, the Luberon Regional Natural Park centre: fossils of fish.*

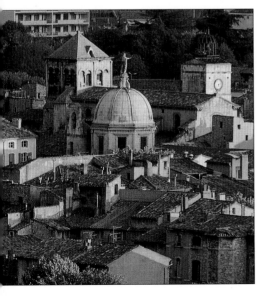

OCHRE COUNTRY

S ituated at the top of a hill, *vicus russulus*, the red mountain, became the village of **Roussillon**. The richly nuanced hues of the ochre quarries which surround it, the Val des Fées (the Fairy Valley), the Falaises de Sang (the Blood Cliffs), the Chaussé des Géants (the Giant's Road), can be found in the roughcast facades of its houses, heightened by the light of dawn and twightlight. About twenty kilometres westward, other ochre quarries were mined, especially at the beginning of the 20th century, in **Rustrel** in an area baptised the Provençal Colorado. In the heart of ochre country, on the the left bank of the Calavon River, **Apt** is the Roman colony *Apta Julia*. During the 3rd century, as a cathedral town, it received the relics of Saint Anne, preserved in the Saint Anne Cathedral, whose construction began in the beginning of the 12th century. During the Middle Ages many pilgrims came here to venerate the relics on view in the upper crypt. The town has a reputation for its production of crystallized fruit and beautiful earthenware, of which many examples are exhibited in the Municipal Museum. But it is also the headquarters of the Luberon Regional Natural Park, created in 1977. Down-river on the Calavon, the Pont Julien was built during the 1st century B.C. in order to allow the *Via Domitia* to cross the river as a connecting route between Spain and Italy via *Apta Julia*.

▲▲ *Cavaillon, the Roman arch. Cabellio, the city of the Cavares, integrated into the Provincia by the Romans, was on the route of the Via Domitia.*

▲ *Cadenet, the drummer of Arcole, a work donated by the artist, André Estienne, to his native city located between Lourmarin and the Durance.*

▲ *Lourmarin. Both Henri Bosco and Camus, who is buried here, loved this village set at the foot of its castle.*

◀ *Cavaillon, Saint Véran Cathedral, the Romanesqu cloister. The cathedral's construction began at the end of the 12th century.*

▶ *The Régalon Gorges. A path explores these gorges carved out by a stream with an erratic rate of flow. It nevertheless managed to carve out a natural tunnel in one area.*

THE LUBERON

For many, the Luberon symbolizes an authentic Provence, a haven and inspiration to numerous artists, painters, sculptures, journalists and writers. It is a limestone anticlinal contained within an elongated triangle with **Cavaillon**, to the west, at its summit and formed by the course of the Durance and the Calavon Rivers. The Luberon Regional Natural Park overflows its natural geographical borders into the plateau of Vaucluse to the north. The **Lourmarin** Comb, which follows the course of the Aigues Brun River, divides the mountain range into two parts: to the east, the Grand Luberon, which reaches its highest point at the Mourre Nègre at 1,125 metres of altitude; to the west, the Petit Luberon. In this still wild landscape, oak, pine, maple and cedar trees grow and reptiles and great birds of prey flourish. Often bathed in a beautiful light, the land is irrigated by several tributaries of the Durance such as the Eze, the Marderic, the Laval or the little Régalon which dug itself a series of gorges. The Luberon is also a wine-producing region, where vineyards profit from the temperate climate in an earth predominately made up of limestone, but also clay, silica and iron. Numerous villages have long been established along this "round back" mountain. Taking advantage of its topography, men settled and built at the top

of a hill here, at the foot of a cliff there, in the dip of a valley or the heart of a vineyard. Isolated and protected by nature, many of these villages served as refuge for the Waldenses, persecuted as heretics. At the end of the 15th century, chased out of the Dauphiné and Piedmont, they joined the migratory flow out of these regions when a demographic explosion tipped the balance economically . Many of these emigrants settled in forty or so villages on the plateau of Vaucluse and the Luberon, such as Gordes, Roussillon, **Oppède**, **Lacoste**, Buoux, **Bonnieux**, Lourmarin, Mérindol. Around 1531, François I engaged in a campaign against heretics and in 1540, the parliament of Provence proclaimed the Mérindol ruling ordering the destruction of this village. Athough it at first escaped, in April 1545, Jean Maynier, the baron of Oppède, heading a veritable army, set fire to and destroyed eleven villages and had their inhabitants shot. Two thousand seven hundred Waldenses were massacred or sent to the galleys. The French monarchy always did pay close attention to what might be smouldering under the embers in this region and in 1660 Louis XIV had the **Buoux** Fort demolished. Today, from the top of its cliff, it provides a magnificent view of the valley of the Aigue Brun . To the north, the plateau of Claperadès, dotted with Bories, slopes down to the banks of the Durance River.

▲▲ *Lacoste.*

▲ *The Buoux Fort. The grain silos of this forteress were carved out of the rock*

◄ *Bonnieux, the church: the Passion, a primitive.*

► *Oppèdes-le-Vieux. The church of Notre-Dame of Alydon and the ruins of the 12th century castle watch over the village.*

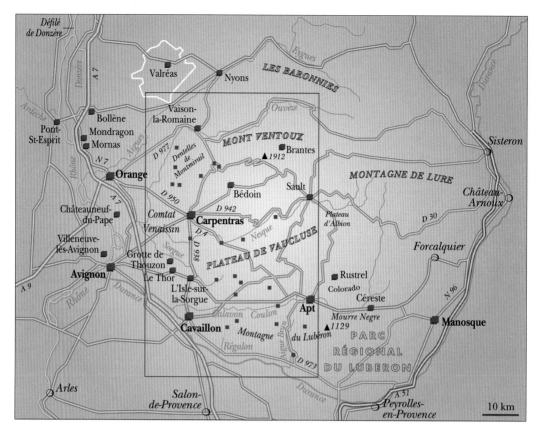

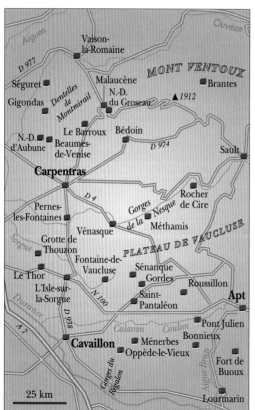

CONTENTS